I Was a Forest

Self-Published

Written and Illustrated by Nathan Harms

Visual Edits by Caleb Harms

ISBN: 979-8-4259-5967-6 (paperback)

ISBN: 979-8-4259-6474-8 (hardcover)

Also available on Kindle

~Contents~

I Was a Forest.... 1

Room 206...11

Halls and Hands.................................19

The Dying Forest.................................27

The Three.................................33

I Ran.................................43

Bee.................................49

The Two Faces of Lament 57

The Monster at the Edge.........................65

In the Morning.................................75

Back the Way We Came.................81

The Wolf.................................89

The Truth.................................97

I... 105

~ Chapter One: I Was a Forest ~

I was a forest. Visceral and magnificent. Respectfully greeting the sunrise as if I were royalty and the skies were my humble and obedient subjects. The heavens bowed to me and my eternal majesty. Confident and poised, beautiful and present.

I was a forest, and the sunset played the role of my canvas while the morning's dawn played the part of my paints. Speckled and random like the thoughts that one might find whilst dreaming.

I was a forest. Beaming with life and innocence, like a child who does not know the pains of an unjust and uncaring world. A world stained in chaos and death, rolling like winds that no one has the right to control. A world with a heart that beats with the reprieve of an aging storm, soon to be gone long before this realm ever knew of its existence.

When I first awoke, I was born to the road that stretched below my wooden limbs. My roots took hold of the rich soil. They grasped to *every* speck of dirt and drank from the waters which resided beneath the world's surface. A drop of life absorbed and swallowed with the warmth of a soft kiss.

I was a forest, full of new life and endless thirst, just born, so therefore viewing the world in bright colors and kind words.

The land where I resided was beautiful and clean. Clear rivers and gorgeous mornings entangled within every single glorious day that I bore witness to. But I was restless, and my mind wandered to the mysterious unknown that existed outside my immediate grasp.

Then as I grew older, I discovered that I could spread my roots and visit new and wondrous places. I could expand my reach and not be trapped by a single range, peak, or land. I could stretch my roots beneath the waves and mountains. Oceans were not walls; they were now roads, and there seemed to be no limits constraining my reach and wonder.

Perhaps, then, I could follow these roots from place to place until finding the perfect home.

I was a forest that wanted their own home but always had one to come back to. I had a dream and was blissfully content with the thought that nothing could ever slow me down.

I was a forest that dreamed and gazed off into deep night skies. I talked with the moon and the stars, and miraculously they seemed to speak back. My imagination ran wild like an orchestra with no conductor, or a storm with no path.

I was a forest. A forest of growth and dreams, which dreamt of a soil that fit me perfectly. A place in which I could grow for miles and have the sweetest of water at the request of a whim. A place that was not accustomed to heavy storms or clouds. A place with streams and sunlight. If such a place existed, then could I not simply just find it? There was no practical reason why such a place could not be my home.

When I was so very young, the elders had informed my thoughts that such a place was incredibly easy to find. For when one is young, their dreams are commonplace to be disproportionately impractical but still fed to them as the almighty truth. But, then as my limbs aged and my mind expanded, the elders informed me that such a place was perhaps unrealistic. Why would they have lied to such a young forest? Did I do something wrong? Maybe I had sprouted the inappropriate sapling at the incorrect time or provided shade on a day in which it was unneeded. Was I now a failure for not being able to obtain my dream of a perfect land in which I could dig my roots deep below the surface?

"Why can I not find this magical land of water and soil, of which I was promised?" I asked the elders.

I was desperate for some kind of answer. Anything was better than not knowing the answers to why my dreams were suffocating under the weight of their aged words and sugared lies.

"Because you were simply much *too* young to know the truth when we told you such foolish things," they replied. "We were just trying to protect you."

Protection can undoubtedly be another word for dishonesty. For if life is about knowledge, then let us feed the brain with all that we have, even if the taste is rather sour.

"So, does not such a place even exist?" I asked.

"We walk *many* paths and grow in *many* directions. The path that we take when first starting our journey, may not be the same one that defines us and our destination," explained the elders.

What a frustrating concept for a forest, such as myself, to learn. To know that my dreams which had sprouted as my roots had grown, were nothing more than a fool's lie. I was simply an anchor held down by the world around me. A slave to these wooden chains that had held me carefully like I was their damaged or untrusting prisoner. Were the words that surrounded me really the truest that could be spoken? Or was this simply a clever joke that was told to me by my elders? Surely, I was more than what I had been promised.

I was a forest. Full of regrets and hopelessness. Having been burdened by the weight of a collapsing dream. Drowning beneath the pressures of a raging and unkind sea. Trapped within the valleys that surrounded my beauty, I attempted to claw my way out of destiny, and find a home amongst the world, no matter what the elders had said. So, I pulled up my roots and slowly made my way to find a better place. Even if such a place did not exist, surely, I could make it appear. I'd will it into existence. I would project such a thing across these bare and open wastelands.

I was a forest, which held on to a dream. A dream of a home that I had imagined since I could barely see. When my eyes were once covered in soil and my lungs had not yet tasted the honey of the air. I held on to these dreams and carried them throughout every single night of unrest. But now was my time to breathe into a future that had tried to abandon me at the crest of every moonrise.

So, I was a forest that had made her way to a haunted land that I hoped I would only call my *"temporary home"*. Or at least it was a momentary place to rest one's weary roots and tired eyes. I yawned. I would only reside in this ghostly place for a couple of days at most. I *would* not, and *could* not, just reside myself to remaining within this place until my dying days. For this place was surely not the place where I was destined to be.

I was a forest, a forest that slowly lost track of time. A forest that never allowed strangers to make camp at their roots. Surely, I was not alone in this lost sense of being. I simply had to be more than what I was. But as the nights and days passed me by, at the pace of blinding light and rushing waves, I found that my roots were starting to tether themselves to the ground, coiling themselves to the haunted soil that slept beneath my feet. They ran deep and held on tightly, never wanting to let go.

I was a forest that had lost all of its precious words. A forest that was starting to also lose all hope. Burdened within the self-realization that my dream was nothing more than a foolish, and childish, notion. And so, I retreated. I slept in the shadows of that haunted place. An unkind and tampered realm of monsters and nightmares. I remained there, for I could not find anything else.

I was a forest, unsure of my future, or if I could ever

grow beyond where I was. I had fallen short of my dreams and fantasies. The stars no longer covered me like a blanket, but instead, the skies were dense and full of grim clouds. The moon fell silent, no longer smiling at me from the night sky.

I was a forest, once. But then I forgot where I came or who I used to be and passed beyond the thoughts of ever finding a home. Drenched in memories and regrets, I retreated to a life of oblivion where I couldn't remember who or what I was.

I was a forest? I think? Wait, how could one person be a forest? That was not practical. Surely, I was not a forest. Surely, I was simply a soul trapped in a city of ghosts and haunted pasts. I just needed a place to lay my head. My mind was fuzzy and confused. My fear led me to the nearest place I could find. A massive structure. So many windows, but no lights. It looked abandoned and forgotten as if lost to the waiting hands of time.

I turned the handle and stepped inside. I was greeted as soon as I walked in the door by, what appeared to be, an old woman who stood behind a colossal wooden front desk, which was covered in a sea of roses that had died on their vine many years prior. Where vines should be, now mold grew. I could not make out the woman's face. She was hidden behind a shadow that my gaze could not pierce through. She seemed not to breathe and stood there silently as if she was made of stone. If not for her obvious shape and long white hair, I might just think that she was simply a strange shadow.

"Hello?" I asked, unsure if she was able to reply or hear me.

There was a cold silence that filled the air.

"What do you want?!" she finally replied in a raspy, and rather annoyed, voice.

Her voice almost sounded as if it were about to give way to coughing with every word that fell from her mouth.

"I… I do not know. I am lost. I used to be a forest, I think… but now I find myself stuck here, without a clear memory of the life I used to lead," I confessed.

"A forest, you say?" the old woman asked with a laugh. "That is preposterous. You were *never* a forest! A forest would not find themselves here, amongst the broken and lost."

"But I swear I once was one… I think. I can *still* taste the water being drunk from the soil, through my countless roots. I can *still* taste the morning air and the waking sun that used to be my breakfast. I *still* feel the joy of watching the seedlings reach for the sky as they took their first breaths," I argued.

"If you were a Forest, then why do you now stand before me as flesh and bone? Tired and confused. Filthy and unclothed. You have abandoned all reason. Why… I bet you don't even know your own name!"

"Of course, I do! I am…"

My mind went blank.

I was a forest.
I was a forest.
I was a forest.

I said it again and again while searching for a name. But I could not find one. And I was slowly forgetting what the sun tasted like. Or what a morning breeze smelled like. It was as if I still remembered most everything from my past life and current thought, but that I was viewing such things through a stranger's eyes.

"Was I a forest?" I asked.

"No," replied the old woman, after a long pause.

How had I arrived here? What was my purpose and place within this frustrating and vague structure? I was so very confused, and the woman behind the counter's words did not inspire much of a direction. But perhaps, she still knew more.

"What should I be doing here?" I asked.

"You are here to sleep. And then wake. And then sleep. And then wake. And so on, until your dying days eventually find you."

The old woman then reached her bone-like hands down below the counter and grabbed a small key, tossing it to me. I barely caught it. I was not used to having hands. At least, it felt like I was not used to it.

"Room 206," she said.

"What?" I asked.

"Go to room 206."

"How do I get there?"

The old woman slowly pointed to an old elevator. It was in the process of being consumed by the walls surrounding it. Moss covered its doors and dust covered its buttons. I made my way over to it, key in hand. After pressing the button to summon its presence, I turned to thank the old woman, but she was gone. The doors opened and I stepped inside.

DREAD

ANXIETY

PASSAGE

DeSTRACTIOn

OBScURetY

DEMiSE

SORrOWFUlNESS

MYStERiES

CATaSTRoPHE

REsT

~ Chapter Two: Room 206 ~

I glanced over the buttons before me.

"What floor is Room 206 on?" I asked myself.

I felt as if I had never been on a contraption such as this before. And yet, I knew that a button must be pressed in order to find momentum, and within so, also destination. Curious.

"Surely it must be on floor two."

But there were no numbers etched across these buttons. Instead, there were seemingly random words stacked atop of one another. Screaming at me to press them, and yet resided to their presence and proper sense. The words that trickled across this panel in front of me seemed *so* random and yet *so* very familiar. Like the feeling of pebbles that one might find under their feet whilst walking across oceans and shores.

DREAD

ANXIETY

PASSAGE

DISTRACTION

OBSCURITY

DEMISE

SORROWFULNESS

MYSTERIES

CATASTROPHE

REST

But which one would lead me to Room 206? I
contemplated this for a moment as the elevator doors
slowly closed behind me. Leaving me in the dark, the
only light within this cage of sliding doors and wires
being the buttons themselves, lit up with a glowing hue of
lime green. I read these destinations aloud. One by one,
weighing the outcomes of any choices that I would
choose to make. It was a nerve-racking affair, filled with
second-guessing and overactive imaginations.

DREAD

No. Simply no. Why would someone press a button that
was marked with the word *"dread"*? Fear, terror, and
trepidation. None of these words warranted a feeling of
cause and reflection to ascend to their mysterious level.
Surely what awaited me on this floor could never be
good. Even speaking the word *"dread"* is not a pleasant
experience for anyone to endure. It is a word that feels
sharp in nature and ugly by design.

ANXIETY

This one made me far *too* nervous to press it. The feelings of unavoidable sadness and stress found their way into my contentious and wallowed thoughts. I had a moment in which I found myself not being able to breathe, and my heart began to echo through my chest like a drum in a canyon. I felt sick. As if I had been clinging to a rejected sense of safety, only to be led to the slaughter of panic. I was simply a sheep, a sheep with no concept of slaughter. No one would choose to climb these floors and gratefully reside on the one named anxiety. Just as no sheep would go where they were told if they knew what the word slaughter meant.

PASSAGE

This did not seem like a destination. Passage of time or through a corridor? A restless word that fell beyond the admiration of an already cluttered and confused mind. It seemed random and vague, glazed in secrets, but not in a pleasurable way. Passage of time is, of course, one of the biggest fears one can wear upon their worried and aged head. Like a crown of thorns that tightens with the movement of seconds and years, slowly bleeding oneself dry. For by the time that you understand what the passing of time entails, you'll most likely be dead and gone, buried beneath the very soil that you had once slept soundly upon.

DISTRACTION

This just seemed like an interruption. A rather silly word. A waste of time. Something that slowly digs deep into one's own mind and embraces itself beneath the curved remembrance of a sunset or dying breath. The world marches on, leaving a distraction of flashing moments stuck within a web of venom and aging lies.

OBSCURITY

Far too vague to be an option. Why would one desire to choose something so riddled with the unknown? Trapped within the pages of shadows and staled progression towards finality. Obscure. Just another word for unidentified. And within this strange and contempt life that we amass familiarity with, why would one choose the unidentified instead of the clarity that might find itself beneath your steps?

DEMISE

This one seemed much *too* obvious to ever dream of pressing. Would you press a button that read; *"certain death to any and all who choose this option"*? Surely not. Surely you would look beyond that option and on to something far more tangible and comforting. Something that would hold you tightly without binding your lungs. Something that would steer you down a path that you could survive. Something, *anything,* other than demise.

SORROWFULNESS

I needed sleep, not tears. I had left my home so very long ago, and I had not slept in many a year. Groggy and weighed down, like mud on one's shoe, simply existing and being drug about as if it was an unwanted appendage. Blank stares hid behind these weary eyes that longed for rest. I would have my day to be sorrowful. But this was not it.

MYSTERIES

This one perplexed me for a moment. Not long enough to persuade my decisions, but long enough to make me question them. Mysteries can truly be an outlier in an otherwise rigged game. Trickled and washed away in questions of greatness or frailty, teetering off the edge of a steep mountain. But silly me, mystery is just another word for obscure.

CATASTROPHE

Who in their right mind would ever press this button? It seemed an obvious choice to me. But what do I know? Simply a lost lamb held prisoner within the shallow choices of buttons and doors.

Surely this was where I was destined to go. If one were to look through this puzzle of words, the only one that would be pressed by choice would be *"rest"*. It was everything that I longed for and desired, wrapped up into one nice, neat word. A word that I couldn't help but whisper. And as it fell from my mouth, it pricked my ears like honey. Sweet and comforting in a way that none of these other buttons had attempted to be. I was sure now. At least as sure as anyone can be when faced with decisions and destinations.

So, I took a deep breath and pushed this button. The button that had seemed obvious but was still shrouded in second guesses. I quickly re-read the other buttons. Had I made the right choice? Had I genuinely thought this through? The little room that I was now trapped in began to move. Racing up this tragic tower and towards a room built on numbers and mystery. But that is where my tired eyes longed to go. Where they needed to go. The elevator shook and sputtered along. Lights flickered and sparks flew. It was almost as if the elevator was starting to speed up. Faster and faster. Spinning within confusion and deep thoughts. An epiphany to the blessed few that cared to push and listen. Then just as fast as it had sped up, this tiny moving room came to an abrupt stop. I stumbled, almost toppling over, but catching myself before I fell. I exhaled, and the doors opened.

It was no longer a matter of correct choices; it was now a matter of consequences. If I had made the right choice, then I would find myself deep within a place of rest. But if I had faltered and made the wrong choice, then I would surely perish under the weight of my decisions. I would be destined to never sleep, to never be at peace, to never be…whom I was meant to be.

206

~ Chapter Three: Halls and Hands ~

As the door opened, I was greeted by the sight of an almost eternally long hall. Its vision was construed and veiled by a thick fog, wrapping itself around the air that poured from my lingering mouth. My mouth was dry, and my throat was heavy. It was as if the fog was pressing down on my airways making sure that I could only just barely breathe. Like the fog was sneaking by my breath, hoping to hide deep within my lungs. It was an unwanted and demented game of hide and go seek.

At the end of the hall, was a dark red door. Like the color of blood. Although I had never seen myself bleed before. If I was to be cut, would not my veins cry of red? Or would they drip sap like a tree that was used to communicate the words of angry men?

I could just barely make out the numbers that hung from the door. 206. This number sang to me. Beckoning me to live within its existence and cling to its every meaning. It meant nothing to me, but I swore it meant more than what it had presented itself as. Shrouded in a comforting mystery and gasping for breath within the fog that clouded my every step.

One step at a time, I started to make my way down this foggy and dimly lit hallway. But as I did so, I began to notice the hallway morph and change, becoming steeper and angrier by the second. Stifled within the negative breath of a demon waiting for me to fall and fail. My stability wavered and broke. It was as if I was walking across a tightrope, unable to maintain my balance, but requiring said balance in order to reach the end of this crooked path.

I walked past door after door, towards my destination. None of the other doors had numbers that made sense to me. It was as if they were scribbled in a different language that no one had *ever* seen before. A language that was lost to the endless seconds of time and space. My imagination told me that they were from a different realm and moment. They almost looked like the drawings of a child. As if the child had been asked to draw a picture of love or whatever emotion that they were holding at the time. Describing said emotion in a picture is much more challenging than one could possibly imagine. Especially if you are so young that the savagery of the world has yet to rear its sharpened fangs at you and reveal itself to your destined future.

I could see those three fated numbers hanging in place as if taunting me with a destination to lay my weary head. They sang to me. Not in a song, but in a radiant chorus that could be felt through the floors and up past my knees. It almost rocked me to sleep. Swaddled in the pull of the vacant sensations that longed to hold me in their waiting arms. Empty and yearning for a sweet and peaceful sleep. The likes of which I had only dreamed of from my last waking moment.

I was… wait, what was I? Ah yes. I was *very* tired. I took step after step towards this destined door that had been justly designed for my tired body. Dry branches and heavy eyes, longing for sweet rest. I passed door after door. Mysterious writings appearing and vanishing with every step. I decided that I would guess what these numbers were. 201,202,203,204,205, and… 206 still seemed so very far away. Why was my restful destination not clinging to my varied steps and finding itself closer to me? Was it just not meant to be? But this is where I knew the elders would have wanted me to go. In turn and step with a self-preserved destination. Unremarkable and predictive to the rains that had laid waste to the lands that I had now forgotten.

  To sleep. To dream. To rest. My head buried deep between fabrics and linens. The smell of lavenders and fine soaps. I could almost taste it. But just as my path was strung across to this quickly approaching destination, a crack appeared in the wall next to me. It was small and unassuming at first but still caught my full attention. It sounded like the snap of a twig within an eerily quiet morning, hypnotizing me to its very existence and tempting my imagination to a myriad of possibilities. Then another crack appeared, and another, and another! Until finally, the cracks shattered like glass and revealed a gaping black hole in place of this once dreary and unremarkable wall. I immediately felt cold and sad, as if a winter chill and a melancholy thought had flown in on the wings of this opening. I dared not look directly into the abyss that lie before me. I turned and glanced at the door at the end of the hall. Warm and inviting. A choice to carry on or let my curious nature demand my steps.

"Eyes forward!" I told myself.

Had I simply just walked forward, then perhaps I would have found myself rested and alive. Awake although stale. The elder's path for me being fulfilled and accepted. But alas, I was too curious. So instead of dragging my feet to room 206, I found myself peering into the darkness of this void and shouting at the top of my lungs.

"Hello!?"

It was silent. All that could be heard was a soft buzzing from one of the hallway lights, jittering, and popping, just barely loud enough to notice. Like a bulb about to die but not ready to accept its fate. I breathed out, slowly looking deeper into this hole, being careful to not lose my footing and fall through. As my eyes adjusted, I could just scarcely make something out. I was not sure what I was staring at, but I did feel its gaze reflecting back at me.

Before my eyes could fully adapt, a hand sprung from the opening and grasped at my face. Lunging at me and trying to choke me. I jumped back out of fear. But then another hand swung at me. And then another, and another. They all looked to be made of rubber. Bending and contorting in ways that did not make sense to me. Not human, not even alive. The skin from these hands hung in place from bone and shadow.

"You deserve your fate," whispered an unseen and unsavory voice.

"What fate?" I asked.

Was I imagining this voice that I had just heard? The hands kept almost leaping at me. Shadows in the dark that longed to cling to my body and pull me away from rest.

"The fate of a forest that flaunts their beauty!" the whisper replied, now slightly louder, as if there was more than one voice speaking.

Clearly, this voice was not born of an overly imaginative mind. I had moved as far away as I could from the portal and hands that were still attacking me. Pressed up against the wall. But the hands seemed to stretch and contort in the most unnatural of ways, inching closer to me.

"But I cannot help my beauty. It is part of who I am. I may not be defined by it, but I do wear it like a heart wears a breath," I replied.

"Just give in to your fate. No need to fight what cannot be stopped. You are *too* weak. And your fate will follow you all your days."

The words from this whisper reflected ominous intentions and threatening eyes. Words like the sharpened teeth of a hungry predator.

"I refuse to accept this fate that you speak of!" I screamed.

"Your fate has already come to pass. Violated and alone, you shall have all your powers stripped from you and *only* death shall remain your friend!" replied the now choir of voices.

The walls shook with this mountain of whispers that were now deciding my apparent fate. Fear overtook me and I suddenly became paralyzed by the madness of more and more hands trying to grab at me. The hallway started to spin, and I found myself finally giving in to the crooked nature of this place and falling to the floor with a loud thud, dropping my key in the process. I felt as if I was just another tree being chopped down in an already forgotten forest.

"You belong to your own regrets now," the whispers said with an eerie laugh.

My eyes grew heavy as I lay there. Then just as the room began to darken, and my mind began to drift from waking to sleeping, I saw hundreds of hands creeping from this shadowed portal and grabbing at my paralyzed body. For all my fear, I could not move. I could not scream for help. I was simply a lifeless body, being pulled gently into the unknown. Slowly drug away against my will. Unsure of what awaited me on the other side of this portal. And then, just like that, everything went dark. The last thing I could remember, was the sounds of whispers and claws, dragging me across the crooked floor, and into the unknown.

~ Chapter Four: The Dying Forest ~

I awoke within a haze, just as I had once dreamt, such a long time ago. I felt the dirt below my hands as my fingers dug deep into the ground, almost as if they were roots. It was as if they longed to burrow deep beneath this particular soil and find a way to quench their unending thirst. But these hands were not roots, not anymore, just as I was no longer a forest. My eyes began to adjust, trying to focus and find a sense of sober clarity. Clouded and almost glued shut by my drying tears and fearful thoughts. How did I end up here? Where was I? The last thing I remembered was a number. A simple number.

"206," I whispered as if reminding myself of what was already known.

I heard my own whisper echo about and rattle around within my weary and compressed head. I was groggy, with heavy eyes and a neck that was betraying the weight of my skull. I felt as if I had been beaten and stabbed, left lifeless but conscious, all at the same time. It was as if I was dreaming, and knew I was dreaming, but no matter how hard I tried, I could not find my way back to the waking world.

Eventually, with a monstrous amount of effort and strength, I was able to focus on the world around me. It was a forest. But not a forest of life and rebirth, no, it was a dead forest. It looked as if its land had been devoured by fire and shadow. Left for dead without a single drop of life to sing to it in the morning's light. The day hid behind a seemingly endless display of gray clouds that colored this lifeless forest with feelings of despair and loss. And yet, there was something *so* very familiar about this place. It was deathly quiet, but I could still almost make out the sounds of my youth. The sounds of hot summers and wickedly cold winters. I could all but remember the fall when this same forest was naked, and the spring, when it was dressed in its most beautiful of gowns. But here it was, in its present state, a shell of its former beauty, a parade of remorse and death. It was as if this place resided in the celebration of its own demise.

But never mind this stranger of a forest that was laced with the familiar. I had to focus on how I had gotten here, and where I was going. I could remember the feeling of being clawed at and scratched by fingers and palms. Hands with no master, pulling me into the eternal void of that mysterious portal. It had been a truly terrifying experience. Had I relived my decisions, perhaps I might have chosen differently and pressed a less obvious choice in that elevator. However, rarely does one think to themselves; "*Rest* sounds nice, but I'd much rather go to the place named *demise.*" One does not think such things, because such things are highly impractical.

I slowly rose above the dirt and mud that lay beneath my tired body. Reaching for a world not of majesty, but of sorrow and lifelessness. I felt alone. Betrayed by my own choices and animosities that had perhaps led me astray. The wind picked up for a brief moment. It comforted me as I tried to rise and stand on my own. It was as if this stiff breeze was attempting to help me to my feet. As I stood and took in the sights of seemingly endless fields of dead branches and rotting stumps, I realized just how much this place *truly* felt familiar. It was as if I was back home but as a different person. A stranger to my own bed. As if my eyes had been betrayed by all the beauty that I knew should be here and replaced with the horrid visions of decay. Was I just seeing what these eyes were allowing me to? Were these trees actually beautiful and colorful? Was this forest actually alive and free? Could it travel to wherever it pleased? Or was it dead and rotting, waiting to catch ablaze and dissolve into nothing but ash, smoke, and a vague sense of familiarity?

The different eyes that I now carried saw this place inversely. The once rosy lens that I had become accustomed to within my youth, was now replaced by a drearier outlook in my older age. I peered around in disbelief, again questioning what I was perceiving. Surely this could *not* be the same forest that I used to call my home. I picked myself up tall and began to make my way through the branches and towards the hopeful warmth of the sun. A sun that seemed to be running away from me as I spent my time chasing it. The branches tore and drug at me. My skin was skewered by the blades of dead tree limbs. Almost in the same way that those faceless hands had clawed at me and ripped me through the darkness. Had these trees sprouted hands and forced me back home?

As I walked further and further, my legs grew even more tired and worn. Then I noticed an odd smell in the air. It was stale and reeked of chemicals and ash. It was hard to breathe but even harder to focus. My mind was sent down a worrying path of fears that sliced and pulled at my endless thoughts until their shape no longer resembled the thoughts of my own. Who had I become? I was destined for a door, but now I was trapped within a sad distortion of my youth. Was I being punished? If so, I would surely be forced to relive my younger days through the haunting spectrum of travesty and loss.

My shadow suddenly seemed to run ahead of me. Maybe it was just the movements of the sun or the fact that dusk was creeping up on me like a predator, ready to pounce and consume its prey. But nevertheless, my shadow did seem to run far away, eventually out of my sight and onto the jealous words and broken hearts that resided beyond my imagination and limited gaze.

"Come back!" I yelled.

I was naturally met with silence, as shadows are not ones for polite conversation. And although I was decidedly certain that it was just my imagination playing tricks on me, I was also aware that I had not seen my own shadow in what seemed to be a very long time. It was as if it had abandoned me. That was quite impractical though. A shadow that runs away. Why that's just pure rubbish! But alas, it truly was gone. It was my only friend. But now it likened the cowards who choose to run away from a subtle storm or a damaged friend.

And so, I was left alone. No shadow. No door awaiting me. No buttons to choose from. Nothing but my gentle breath to keep me company. I hung my head in sadness. And then in that same sadness, I was suspended for what felt like hours and hours. Perhaps days, or weeks, or years! There was no way to be sure. The days stretched long, and the years passed by. I was left in the cold, weathered, and yet not withered. It had to have only truly been moments, but it felt like an eternity.

Then after all this time had passed, my throat suddenly closed, and my breath stopped. The gentle breeze that had certainly been somewhat present, disappeared. There was no sound. Nothing. I lifted my head. And came face to face with fear.

~ Chapter Five: The Three ~

Behold the three.

   Three entangled ghostly figures now appeared before me. Suspended within the echo of a shadow. I found that I was not quite face to face with them as they were thinly veiled and shielded in the cloak of a haunted mystery. They almost waltzed with me and my wavering movement, as if connected to my every breath. But these were not my shadow, for my shadow had run away. No, these were the shadows of something that closely resembled death. The death of innocence and pride. The shadows of evil men that had been before and would be again. I knew in my heart what their true names were. The Withered, the Ravenous, and the Wolf.

   The Withered still hung onto some pale shape of their former self. Retaining the commonplace of childlike innocence. Even though this innocence was buried far below the surface of what this soul now was. They knew the wrongs of the world but chose to ignore them and push far beyond their compass of morals and lies. Their inner voice was slowly eating away at them, from inside, gnawing at their flesh like a lion enjoying its most decadent of kills. All that could be seen of their former self was the two white stars that now resided where their eyes used to dwell. A haunting reminder that even the vilest of monsters are destined to begin this life as a child. These eyes were the only real reflection of the human side to this shadow. A body that was now withered and left behind. But the Withered did still remember this body and soul. And therefore, was the only one of these creatures that were worthy of *any* type of understanding.

The Ravenous had given up on their moral self, many years ago. Their childlike morality died the day they took their first breath. The rarest of souls, actually born evil. They did not feel the need to placate their apathy by nature. Instead, they stuck to the corners and made jokes about the victims that had been left behind. Victims like me that had been shrouded in their laughter. No one knew this pain like me. The suffering. But the Ravenous does not care. They know the truth behind their actions but choose to not do anything about it. There is no conflict for the Ravenous. Only apathy and selfishness. Untrustworthy and as vile as they come. Truly finding pleasure in others' pain. No rest for the wicked, and no work for the damaged.

Lastly, the Wolf. The silent killer. There is no right or wrong to them. They are not aware of the callus nature that masks their ways. They care not for the screams or the mastered buckling of knees and weak palms that they leave behind. They kill innocent shadows and rip them from the halls. Animal-like in nature, their natural instincts as an apex predator. Pruning innocence and burning dreams. Should you ever find yourself at a doorway, beware the Wolf, for there will be no escaping them and their hunger. They will tear you to shreds and never let you be. Choosing to follow you into your waking nightmares and pick away at your bones until there is nothing left.

"We are so *very* glad to see that you have finally arrived," said the Wolf in a voice that resembled a dying man on his death bed. As if every single forced word might be his last.

"You look like a fool!" yelled the Ravenous with a shrieking voice, like a banshee screaming to the heavens.

"You look tired," moaned the Withered in a sad, deep voice.

"You look weak," whispered the Wolf.

They were all well beyond the obviousness of how I was feeling. As if they had peeled open my skull and read my thoughts like a novel.

"I am all that you have said and more," I finally replied.

Although their faces were notably vacant behind the shadows that they wore, I felt a familiarity with these monsters that hovered before me. It was not a kind-hearted familiarity, but more like the knowledge of a painful death. You are aware that it is real, but most would choose to not befriend it.

"How is it that I know your names?" I asked.

The Wolf laughed ever so slightly. They had no intention of answering my questions of familiarity.

"Are you not frightened of us?" asked the Ravenous. They chuckled a little after asking this question. As if this was entertaining for them to watch me relive my pain, squirming and shivered.

"I am not!" I yelled defensively, immediately knowing that I was screaming a lie. "I know *who* you are! I know *why* you are here!"

"And *why* are we here?!" asked the Wolf.

"To infect me with shame! To destruct my very being with guilt and regret!" I replied.

"Do you not believe in shame?" asked the Withered.

"I… I do not know!" I stuttered.

My thoughts went to the feelings of shame that had started to creep over me. It felt like a spider on the back of your neck, slight tickles that at first, you could swear were just your imagination. Until that venomous bite exposes your truth. I was not supposed to fear these three evils that hovered before me. I had sung a chorus of such promises. No fear. No shame. But their very presence tugged at my emotions and slowly drove me to a point where I had to second guess my own song. My mind screamed at me, telling me that there was nothing to feel shameful about. But nevermore could my chorus be heard.

"She feels it," remarked the Ravenous.

"She regrets it," said the Withered.

"She hates it!" screamed the Wolf.

"I… I do not know what I feel," I replied. "Why must I always know what I feel?!"

"Because you feel a great shame," said the Wolf. "You feel that you should not reside in the lands of your youth. You can see these lands clearly with your new eyes. You now see them through a veil of pain. Worthless and strung out for the world to see. We have put you on display, like a freak in a sideshow."

"Come one, come all!" screamed the Ravenous.

"But why is any of this my fault? I did not choose to surrender myself to the portal in the hall. I did not choose for those cold hands to claw and grab at me, dragging me into this place. It was not my fault!" I yelled.

"But was it not your choice to be there? Was it not your choice to press the *easy* button? Many choices had laid before you. But you chose the one that felt as if its pain would not be present," replied the Wolf.

"Might we just let her be? Hasn't she suffered enough?" asked the Withered.

"Fool!" screamed the Ravenous. "That is just like your being. Withered and yet alive. Clinging onto a fabricated morality. Do not try to act a saint when it was your hands, as much as mine, that drug her here."

"But I do feel shame," confessed the Withered.

"NO! You do not!" screamed the Wolf.

It was as if the three had forgotten my very existence as I swayed in their shadows. They then started to argue with each other as to who deserved to be praised.

"It was all my brilliance that brought her here," the Ravenous said smugly.

"You dare take ownership of my rightful royalty. My crown! My throne!" yelled the Wolf.

"Perhaps your throne should no longer belong to you!" said the Ravenous.

"Perhaps I shall cut you down to nothing!" the Wolf howled.

The Ravenous and the Wolf continued to bicker with one another as to who was more powerful. They cherished the title of the evilest and most foul. Suddenly, the Withered began to float towards me. I was frightened at first. I could still feel their cold hands as they had traveled the lands of my body. Shameful or not, this disgusting soul should not be trusted.

"I am truly sorry for what we have done to you," said the Withered rather timidly.

"And just why should I forgive you?!" I yelled.

"Please, try and remain quiet. I do not want my brothers to hear you."

"You have not answered my question. Why should I forgive you?" I whispered.

It was a whisper that was drenched in anger and hate. Had you heard this whisper you would shiver at the sharp squeal of these breathy words.

"I do not require or ask for forgiveness. I will live with my shame for all my remaining days, taking it far beyond a nameless grave. I only hope that you can find a way to stretch beyond these horrendous crimes and find your leaves in the basking warmth of the sun once again."

Tears began to stream down my face. I was overcome with a sadness that one might find in the endless rains of funerals. I wanted to feel the sun again, but from where I now stood, it seemed impossible. I could not fathom a reality in which I could feel whole again.

"And just *how* am I supposed to do that?" I asked.

"Follow the path ahead. Do it while my brethren are distracted so you do not have to face them. On that path, you will encounter *more than four but less than five* strange beings."

More than four but less than five? I was bewildered by this statement but simply chose to accept it as the fact between the breath.

"These are creatures unappreciated and cast out. Misunderstood as yourself. Find them and listen… and you will then find peace."

I turned and looked at the road before me. The torment of these three evil beasts, shrouded in shadows, was far too much for me to endure. I had to take the path that the Withered had proposed.

"If I take this road, I shall still not forgive you," I said.

"As I have already stated. I do not want forgiveness. Just pray for me."

"Very well. What type of prayer do you request?" I asked.

"Pray that hell is kind to a monster like me."

And so, I disappeared deep into the forest, towards the path that the Withered had instructed that I take. I evaded the eyes of the Ravenous and the Wolf. Their still arguing voices trailed off, buried beneath the rotting stench of what I now perceived as a dying forest. Perhaps my new path would lead my eyes to see this place in a better light. After all, a journey often reminds us of truths.

~ Chapter Six: I Ran ~

I ran.
I ran as fast as I could.
As far as my legs would carry me.

Tight and narrow, the path of Gods and men are in reality the same. They make you feel bare and naked. Vulnerable and sick. Your feet are not aware of the ground that they seem to float across. Like waves on a bitter ocean, mesmerized and drowning beyond the limits of an already damaged and broken mind. This path was for the unwelcomed. But who else does the path consume and travel besides? The elderly and damaged. The young and lost. People from all walks of life who have lost the direction that was once painted before them. Their song has been re-written and replaced with a melody that does not sound like the song that they once knew so well. Inscribed like the voice of their mother, singing, and weeping in the dead of night. Beyond the witching hour is where this path leads all that choose to follow.

So now I traveled this path myself. But was I a victim? Was my willingness to try and defy the will of my elders the reason that I had been drug here? I kept playing out the moments again and again. A dark hall with a flicker of light, buzzing and hissing at me as I made my way to room 206. All I wanted was rest. All I desired was time. Time to clear my weary head and dream. Ah yes, to dream.

I had often thought about my dreams. My dreams taunt me and haunt me like a restless spirit. They are what cause me to crave sleep. For only in dreams was my life fully realized. Only there could I see my face again.

I was a… I forget.

But never mind.

Even if I could remember, why would I ever choose to burden the world with a title that I was not strong enough to hold on to? I did not deserve it. Filth. I was an animal. No, I must not do that. I must blame the three, *not* myself. But it is hard to blame others even when it is practical to do so. We are raised to not blame others for our problems. But would you not blame the man holding the knife if he were to stab the stranger?

The path before my feet was rippled like a stream. And just like a stream, I was pulled along. It was as if my legs were just being tugged by an unseen force. All I could see around me for miles was dust and ash. The night sky was devoid of stars. No light or reprieve could be seen in the distance. Why was I traveling a path that only led me further into emptiness? A place where I could not speak to the moon and stars, or travel hallways in search of rest.

In the farthest distances, I could just barely make out a tree line. It was just beyond my sight, almost hidden by the blanket of shadows that hung from the night sky. The trees appeared to almost glow with a white light that neither comforted nor scared me. It just was. And when something simply is, then one should not question its right to exist.

As the tree line began to get closer to me, I started to hear something. It sounded like a storm. At first quiet. But then it began to grow louder. It was coming from where I had just been but was heading towards where I was now going. It was as if the storm was chasing me, living in my every thought, and surrendering itself to the might and fear that poked at my back. It was like a downpour of needles, haunting me and degrading my every breath. I dared not look behind myself for fear of what I might see.

But after the winds began to stab at my arms and legs, I had no choice but to surrender to my curious nature and bow before the royalty of knowing. As I turned my head slightly, I could see the Wolf and the Ravenous, flying towards me with a mountain of dark clouds attached to their floating heels. They were coming after me. They both howled and shrieked. My heart began to race and bounce about my chest. I had no control over how fast this stream was moving me down this path. And although the tree line seemed to be growing closer, I feared that I might not outrun this storm before being sheltered in the arms of the forest's possible safety.

I looked forward, intent on surviving this now unsettling journey that I was being led on. As the white forest got closer and closer, I could hear the whispers of the Wolf close to my ear. I could feel their rotting breath trying to mock me. I could smell their stench and I dared not look around for I did not want to come face to face with my attackers again. I would not face them. I chose to leave their foul teeth behind me, being tossed about by the breeze of their own storm.

"Shame!" they both screamed.

Hissing and snapping could be heard and felt at my feet. I was close now, but I was fearful that I was *not* going to make it. Safety was not going to find me on this day. Even after the Withered had tried to steer me into a direction of comfort and freedom, what would stop these monsters from not simply just following me into this new forest?

But then, as I approached the tree line, almost hidden in its shadows, a low rumble began to shake the ground. It was not unpleasant to my own ears, but I could tell that the monsters and their storm were suddenly halted in place. I could feel fear at my back. I could feel safety in my future. What was it that had stopped these monsters in their place? What could have possibly made me feel safe enough to look behind me and trust my path's journey? As I turned to look at my past, I could see the Wolf and the Ravenous as they sulked away, back to that lifeless place where they had come from. They howled and screamed as if they had just lost their most delectable reward.

Eventually, I found my feet planted firmly back on the ground, resting atop the softness of this new soil. I looked around. My curious nature needed to know what had saved me at that last instant. What had heard my beckoned calls and soft whimpers and decided that mine was a life worth saving?

This forest was far different from where I just was in my immediate past. It was blinding in its radiance and beauty. The white trees glowed like a pale sun. I felt peace. Not happiness, but peace. There is a subtle difference, and I could feel it. I will compare it to the following: it felt like hugging a stranger who would never be made aware of how much their embrace meant to you on *that* day, at *that* time. Perhaps the embrace transpired on a heartbreaking day in which someone you genuinely cared about had passed away. At that moment, a soft hug could be incredibly comforting and bring you peace, even if it does not bring you joy. And that stranger would have no idea just how much that hug would now mean to you. Until your dying breath, you would always remember the kindness of that stranger, yet they would have almost immediately forgotten all about that momentary embrace.

So, like a stranger's embrace, I felt the soft winds push at me, directing my steps. I knew where I was meant to walk towards. I could see a tree. It was hollowed and dark inside of its bark barricades. Then I heard a familiar low rumble reverberating from within. That same low rumble that had spared my catastrophic life. It was like stepping into a shadow. But amidst the darkness, there was a soft and inviting feeling. And so, I held my breath and stepped inside.

~ Chapter Seven: Bee ~

Inside this mysterious husk of a tree, I found a peculiar creature, the likes of which one cannot define but must see to believe. I could not tell whether they were made of skin or bone, or maybe even some combination of the two. If both were present, I was unsure of how to tell where one stopped, and the other began. I approached this creature with great caution. I had just, after all, come face to face with monsters of immense evil and danger, and one can never be too cautious when approaching creatures that cannot be described. As I approached, they turned their head and stared at me. At least I thought that they were staring at me. Their eyes were hollow like the skull of someone who had died many centuries ago, and I could almost hear the winds echo from inside this creature's seemingly empty head.

"Hello there," the creature said in a low, yet oddly friendly, voice.

"Um…I."

I did not know how to reply. This creature did not seem terrifying within their words, but ironically comforting with their tone. Like a dark cloud that only gives way to light rain. And while normally one tries not to use words such as *goofy* or *silly* when describing things such as voices, actions, or creatures, there was truly only one way to describe this creature's low voice. Silly.

"You seem sad. Would you like to hear a joke?" they asked.

"I… sure," I replied, still in shock over this strange creature's bizarre tone and features.

"Knock… knock," they started.

I knew this one. These were *never* actually funny. Should this strange creature end up not as a jester, but as a sad excuse for a laugh?

"Who's there?" I replied.

"Boo," they said with a little chuckle.

"Boo, who?" I said, ready for the all too predictable punchline.

"You seem sad. Would you like to hear a joke?" they asked.

"I…"

"Knock… knock," they started again.

"Who's there?"

"Boo," they said with another little chuckle.

I simply couldn't help but chuckle back at them a little.

"Boo, who?"

"You seem sad. Would you like to hear a joke?"

"So, round and round we go? Is that your game? Are you some form of clown?" I asked.

They stared at me in silence.

"I will not start your joke again," I said with a little laugh. "You are a silly creature."

"Then my joke worked," they finally replied.

"And how *exactly* did it work?" I asked.

"Well… you did laugh."

Perhaps this strange creature had a point. Their adolescent attempt to make me crack a smile had certainly succeeded in the slightest of ways. My belly did not jiggle from laughter, but my cheeks were raised. A smile and a giggle. This was the first time, in what felt like forever, that I had not felt sadness or shame. In fact, I started to almost feel like a child.

"Well then, I thank you," I said. "What is your name?"

"A name? Why, I have no name," said the creature, with an almost rigidly practical tone. As if I should just know for a matter of fact that they did not possess a name.

"No name? That is very strange."

"Would you like to name me? Perhaps something silly or whimsical," they suggested.

"Hmmmm, fine. Then I shall name you, Bees' Knees," I proclaimed.

"Ah yes. You may call me Bee for short," Bee replied.

"Very well, then, Bee. What are you doing out here?" I asked.

"I was waiting for a sad soul. A sad soul that I could temporarily make smile," said Bee.

"Well, I guess you have now done that. But why?" I asked. "My problems are still here. Even now I can feel them sneaking back up on me like a sunrise sneaks up on the morning."

"Because," Bee began. "A smile is the only force strong enough in this uncaring world to alleviate the saddest of hearts, even if it is just for the briefest of moments."

"But if it's just for a moment, why bother?"

  Bee stared at me for a moment. Unblinking, unwavering. Then blew a raspberry (which naturally caused me to smile) and then proceeded to respond to my question.

"Life is just a series of moments. Smile enough, and it'll end up that a fair amount of your life is spent being happy."

  Bee was correct. I was haunted by terrible things. Hands in a hall and three monsters in a dying forest. It was enough to cause anyone to give up and choose to never smile again. But why had I not given up? Certainly, I had felt close to such a thought. But my mind had undoubtedly changed over the last several moments. I *still* felt sadness, but it was laced with the smallest bit of bliss.

"You have certainly made me happy for a moment. And I do wish that this could go on for longer. But sadly, I cannot stay," I said.

"You needn't stay to feel happy," replied Bee. "You can take my silly jokes and soothing voice wherever your travels take you."

"And just how can I do that?" I asked.

From seemingly nowhere, a waltz began to play. It was soft and simple, with strings out of tune and an apparently broken-sounding drum. It was silly, and bizarre, and I had no idea where this strange music was coming from. And then Bee cleared their throat and started to sing a little song. Their voice was horribly out of key, but it did make me laugh.

"You simply have to
sing a little song,
or dance a little dance,
tell a little joke,
or put on a pair of pants!"

"What's so funny about putting on pants?" I asked, halting the song for a moment.

"It's funny if you put em' on backwards!" Bee replied with a laugh.

The waltz then continued, and Bee stood up and started to do a little dance. It was not a good dance. It wasn't even really a dance. It was more like; Bee hadn't stood up in a million years and was simply stumbling around. The song continued.

"You simply have to
play a little game,
or tell a silly joke,
laugh a little laugh,
or give a little poke!"

"And how *exactly* is giving someone a little poke funny?" I asked.

Bee immediately took their long boney arms and poked me in my stomach. It made me laugh a little, and then a lot, and then I was laughing so hard that I found myself on the ground, almost in tears.

"See, that's how it can be funny!" Bee said.

And then, as I regained my composure, Bee launched into what must have been the grand finale… and hopefully *not* just another verse.

"This is life, and you better love it!
When we are sad, we rise above it!
You better laugh like there's no tomorrow!
It's the best way to ease your…"

Bee looked at me, note holding, imaginary band still playing, waiting for a reply. I was put on the spot. What rhymed with tomorrow? Buffalo? Eskimo? Big toe? And then it came to me.

"Sorrow!"
I sang loudly before surrendering to a fit of laughter.

It felt good to laugh again. It felt good to be alive. And even though I was positive that *the three* would show their evil again, and that my problems were not gone for good, they were gone for a moment. Laughter is a funny thing. Like a clown without a circus or a jester without a court, Bee sat back down and silently returned to sitting still, waiting for another sad soul in need of a laugh. I could feel that it was my time to move on. An end of a moment, shrouded by a blissful backdrop of temporary happiness. A silly song and a bad joke. Honestly, not the worst legacy to leave behind. And as I looked back at Bee, sitting there silently, I couldn't help but think; I am surely happier now than I have been in an exceedingly long time.

~ Chapter Eight: The Two Faces of Lament ~

As I walked alongside this shimmering forest, I began to notice the glow subsiding. Gone was the essence of the new, and the safety of the unknown. Now I was left with a forest that once again looked drab, dreary, and unapologetically lifeless. It was as if my outlook had followed me across fields and oceans, leaving my eyes deadened to any sort of life or rebirth.

Suddenly, I came upon another strange creature. It shared the same hollow-looking eyes that had belonged to Bee. Its body was contorted and misshapen, like a flightless bird with no feathers. It was slightly taller than me, and although it was not frightening at first, it then turned its head to reveal another face. A face made of sharpened teeth and rotting branches. No eyes could be seen on this other face, only darkness. Like a void of eternal nothingness.

At first, this creature did not notice me, and for fear of being killed or attacked, I was content with this fact. After all, this creature did seem like a rather obvious metaphor for fear. But as I tried to sneak away, unheard or seen, I saw the creature trip on their own arms and get stuck in a patch of sinking sand. They began to flail about and scream wildly. Admittedly, I had pondered the act of running away and evading my eyes from the travesty that this two-faced creature was presently enduring. But that was not the kind of soul that I was raised to be. I cared. Sometimes to my own detriment.

I ran towards the creature and without even thinking, I grabbed hold of them and ripped them from the ground's grasp and to safety. It was *not* easy and required all the strength that I could summon from my already exhausted body. We both fell to the ground, depleted, trying to catch the breath that clung to the thick air.

"Are you okay?" I asked, unaware if this creature could even understand me, let alone talk.

"I am as I was before… almost dying… alive but in despair," the softer of the two faces replied in an almost whisper.

The creature slowly brought themselves to their feet, dusting themselves off and trying to regain their composure,

"Why did you save us?!" yelled the second face with a hiss and a low growl.

For ease of story and comprehension, I will confess now that I never asked these strange creatures, or creature, their name. But since I do not want to lose your wandering eyes, I will name them: Face 1(for the soft, albeit sad face) and: Face 2 (for the angry face). I chose to assign these numbers due to the amount of respect that

I had for each one of these strange personalities that resided atop this odd bird-like creature.

"Do not scold her!" Face 1 said to Face 2.

"And why should we not scold her?! We don't like being alive anyway. The sinking of sands seemed like an exceptionally fine way to go!" yelled Face 2.

"Oh, I am *so* very sorry that I rescued you then," I interrupted, slightly sarcastic and annoyed. "Sincerest apologies."

"Oh, dear. It is quite alright. Please ignore my *lesser* half. A backside that is never happy," said Face 1.

"A backside that always has your back, you mean," grumbled Face 2.

"Do you not both get along with each other?" I asked innocently as if this would simply be common and obvious knowledge.

"Oh yes, we get along just fine," answered Face 1.

"Why would you think we didn't get along?!" yelled Face 2.

"You must not be *very* observant if you think that we don't get along," said Face 1.

"You must not be *very* smart to think that we don't get along," said Face 2.

I was taken back by their dedicated objection to any type of indifference or delusion. As if the very suggestion that they did not get along was too massive a concept for them to imagine.

"I just thought…" I started.

"Thought what?!" yelled Face 2.

"Let her speak," yelled Face 1.

"Oh, shut up!" argued Face 2.

"See, that, right there. You're yelling at each other. That's why I thought you didn't get along," I said.

Face 1, the only one with any form of eyes, looked over at me puzzled.

"Do you think because we speak at different volumes, that we don't get along?" they asked.

"Well, no. It is also what you say. The words contained within your volumes speak of conflict with one another," I said.

"Ah yes. That is a particularly good point," said Face 1.

"No, it's not!" argued Face 2.

"You see, we are the two faces of lament," started Face 1. "Myself, I am rather sorrowful and sad all the time. I am burdened by my past and future. I have a tough time seeing anything good in nothing bad. So, I am how I am. Whereas my other half is…"

"I am angry!" yelled Face 2. "I am also sorrowful and sad all of the time. But instead of sulking about, I am mad about all that I cannot change and all that I can!"

"But if you are both unhappy, which way of feeling sad is the correct way?" I asked.

"Neither!" replied Face 1.

"Both!" replied Face 2.

The forest went quiet at that point. The stale air trying to break within the silence to an orchestra of the uninspired and dull. I cleared my throat as I thought of what I should say next. There was *clearly* no right or wrong way to reply. But then it came to me.

"Ah, yes! I think I understand!" I said somewhat excitedly.

"Doubtful," mumbled Face 2.

"When it comes to being sad," I started. "There is no

right or wrong way to feel or be. You simply are. One may be sad and depressed. Trapped inside their own mind, with no intention to ever share their deepest depressions and thoughts. Or you may be angry and loud. Positive of your reckoning and outlook. Stringing words like harsh winds all about the world. Neither way is positive or good. But both are required on the road to acceptance."

"I did not understand a word you just said," whispered Face 1.

"Finally! Something upon which we can agree!" yelled Face 2.

I chuckled to myself. I had found a little bit of a smile with Bee. Their humor was dependent upon my steps and had followed me to this moment. I realized that when sad, you do not see what face you are wearing. Two ways to deal, neither wrong nor right, just there. And that's okay. What matters, is that if you have two faces of lament, do not assume that these two faces cannot coexist with one another. Instead, realize that both faces are needed in order to deal with the melancholy. One face might be louder or talk more. But both are needed.

And with that, I went about my way. I traveled away from those two faces and onward towards the outskirts of this new forest. I was not sure where I was heading. But I could feel myself being drawn towards something. Some type of destination that was both familiar, and mysterious.

~ Chapter Nine: The Monster at the Edge ~

The trees and limbs of the forest began to clear, and I found myself walking into an endless abyss of white. It was as if I was traveling through a cloud, strolling along the boundless oblivion of the heavens. But before the trees had completely left my side, I met yet another strange creature. A giant. A colossal thing. Massive in size and strength, it echoed over my very existence. Its multiple legs and arms were almost sown into the ground itself, melting into the soil. It bore the same hollow eyes of those whom I had met before and was made up of what looked to be silhouettes and shadows. Sharpened teeth pierced the breath that surrounded it.

Surely, it would be wise to sneak past this shadowed monster and onward towards the pale oblivion. But as I left the forest, I found that every step I took was paired with the sound of thunder. It was as if my feet had grown incredibly heavy and large, with each movement bringing forth a symphony of drums. The ground seemed to shake with every movement that I found myself being part of. I hoped that this beast had not noticed the cavernous sounds erupting from my steps. But as I peered upwards towards this monster, I found that not only had it heard the sound of my steps, but it was looking right at the source of those responsible. Its giant, hollowed, and unblinking eyes stared directly at me, focused on my stilted breath. The beast leaned down towards me, inches from my face. Its cold breath made my hair bounce and fly.

"I…I'm sorry to have disturbed you," I stammered, shaking in place, and filled with fear of this beast.

"You are *very* beautiful," the monster said.

Their voice was very loud, but also incredibly soft and kind. Not the sort of voice that one would expect to hear from such an unbelievably massive creature. Theirs was a voice of endless comfort and care.

"Um, thank you," I replied, unsure if that was the right response to give.

"You are quite welcome," they replied.

They then took a massive breath, breathing right into my face. But where one might think that the breath of a monster would be incredibly hot and vile in stench, I was pleasantly surprised to find their breath chilling and soft. It also smelled of peppermint and chocolate.

"Why are you so small?" the monster asked.

"Why are you so big?" I replied with a bit of a chuckle.

"You really are *very* beautiful," the monster repeated.

I found it odd that this massive creature just kept summarizing my beauty. I wondered if perhaps there was a far more nefarious intention behind their honeyed words.

"Are you going to eat me?" I asked calmly.

The creature recoiled back as if shocked by such a crass allegation.

"Am I going to what?!" they replied.

"Eat me? You know, consume me for sustenance and nourishment?"

"Why I never!" they yelled.

"I'm sorry. I did not mean to offend you. You are just very monstrous and keep commenting on my beauty. My past forced me to assume that you had ulterior motives."

The monster was silent for a moment as if thinking of their response. Tongue-tied and awkwardly speechless, being careful to craft the perfect reply.

"Hmmmm," they finally responded after a rather long time. "I have no intention of eating you. I, myself, am a *watertarian*."

"A watertarian? You mean…"

"Yes, I only drink water," they said.

"Well, that is good to know. I am sorry for being so untrusting."

The monster almost seemed to smile. It was, however, quite off-putting given their crooked and sharp teeth that bulged from their head.

"It is quite alright. What is your name, ma'am?" they asked.

"I was a…"

My mind went blank, and I could not find the words that I *so* dearly wanted to exhale out into the world.

"I do not know," I finally replied.

"Hmmmm, well, my name is Norman."

"Norman?!" I asked while irrupting in laughter.

"Yes, Norman! What's so funny about the name Norman?"

I abruptly stopped laughing and tried to control myself. I, after all, did not want to hurt the feelings of this monster that could easily eat me, even though they much preferred the taste of water to flesh.

"Nothing is funny about it," I assured Norman. "It is just a *very* tame name for such a *very* scary and powerful-looking creature such as yourself."

"Ah, yes but looks can be deceiving. You assumed that I would eat you because I was kind to you. You assumed that I was a monster because I was taller than you. You assumed that you needed to fear me before you knew my name. My guess is, that you had judged me *before* you knew me."

"I've had terrible experiences with monsters made of shadows before," I confided.

"I can see that. And that is why I am not offended by your caution. You may live the rest of your days with the taste of prudence falling from your lips. You may not respond to compliments with innocence and open arms. But rest assured, that *is* okay. There is nothing wrong with being untrusting. So long as once you learn the monster's name, and that they are a watertarian, you relax your sword and attempt to look beyond their surface."

"That is fair," I said while smiling.

We talked long into the day of all things past, present, and future. It turned out that Norman loved to sing. However, whenever he did so, the rest of the creatures that lived here just assumed that it was a distant storm, cracking and ringing high up in the heavens.

"I never have had a very good singing voice," laughed Norman.

"Then why sing?" I asked.

"Because… I love to sing."

Such a simple reply to such an obvious question. *Because they loved to sing.* Maybe I should adopt some of those same traits in my life. Do things because of passion, not due to commands or expectations. True, I would have still found myself in that hall. But, perhaps after my ordeal, I would not have stayed stranded in the dead forest of self-shame for as long as I had.

As the sun began to set, I decided that it would be best to make camp here with Norman. I had not seen the stars in many years, and perhaps I could even say hello to my old friend the moon.

"Is it alright if I remain at your side until tomorrow morning?" I asked.

"It would be my honor, ma'am."

I smiled at Norman. A creature of whom I had cast judgment upon but came to find my heart entangled within their majesty and kindness.

"I am sorry again for judging you before knowing you," I said as my eyes grew heavy and as I laid upon the ground, almost immediately drifting off to sleep.

"Do not be sorry. For in a world full of evil, I am the one that is sorry that you have to be cautious and untrusting."

I had not truly slept since before I had arrived at that cursed hotel. Since before I had taken that steel trap to the floor of rest. Since before I was drug to the dead forest. I had not rested. But in the shadow of a beast named Norman, I slept. Comfortable and content for the first time since I had been broken so severely.

"Would you like me to sing to you?" the beast whispered as I surrendered to my exhaustion.

I nodded just as I was pulled deep into my dreams. The last thing I remembered was the ground vibrating under the song that Norman sang. Slow and beautiful, rocking me to sleep and silencing all the demons of the past.

That night I dreamt of going home. Of seeing it through brightened eyes, and therefore, how it truly was. Beautiful and in bloom. Flowers and fruit dripping from limbs and songs of life flowing throughout the air. I just had to return to my home. I knew that I would not be returning as the person that I once was. But I had no choice. We carry the scars that are inflicted upon us by a cruel and uncaring world. They define us. They burden us. But it is *our* choice what we choose to do with them. Do we simply allow them to play the role of our anchor, forever tying us to the melancholy? Or do we carry their weight upon our back and hope that given time, their influence becomes less?

I will carry these scars upon my back and head home. I will turn around and face those who have hurt me. I will *not* forgive, I will destroy. I will laugh in their faces by choosing to live the life that I should have lived all along. I will no longer be controlled by their evils.

I remembered back to when I was young. And as I slept soundly, I repeated the following in my head again and again until the sun rose high up in the sky, greeting me and vowing to help me face my scars.

I was strong.

I was beautiful.

I was life.

I was love.

I was a forest.

~ Chapter Ten: In the Morning ~

I rose to meet the sun, basking in the warm glow of the heavens. What had changed? Surely it was not just Norman's company and song. Nor was it the two faces that had taught me how to grieve, or Bee's jokes and laughter. But, perhaps, it was some strange combination of all these things.

"Norman?" I asked softly.

My eyes adjusted to the morning's light. My sight was blurred and also beckoned to awaken my own existence. I looked upwards to greet Norman, only to find that there was no one there. No shadowed beast that had watched over me as I slept and sang those sweet earth-tremoring songs. I was saddened by this. Had they abandoned me? Was I still a, wait, what was I? So many steps forward. So much power beneath every single one of those steps. But I was. I was…

"You were a forest," said a small voice.

I turned to find myself staring at a tiny and unassuming creature. Their eyes looked familiar. And their teeth were revealed, although *very* dull. They seemed to be made not of shadows, but bone, and yet, they were still somewhat attached to the soil of which they stood atop.

"Norman?!" I asked somewhat suspiciously.

"Good morning, ma'am," they said while slightly bowing.

"But were you not just towering above me and made from shadows and songs?"

Norman bounced about and danced around me while ignoring my question. Full of energy and life. As if being fueled by the light brought forth by the sun and morning.

"The morning seems to have been kind to your once deadened eyes. Can you now see things clearly?" they asked.

"Perhaps I can," I replied.

I was perplexed by Norman's now minuscule height. Did my eyes just deceive me in the moon's light? Was I talking to a tiny creature and not a massive beast all along?

"Were you always this size?" I asked.

"Not in your eyes. You see, you encountered me as a broken and abundantly cautious casualty. Assuming that I would harm you and leave scars. I towered over you so that you could find fear and run away if necessary. Your defense was your eyes, and your concern was your heart."

"You will meet more than four but less than five," I said to myself.

"What was that?" Norman asked.

"Nothing, just the end to a peculiar mystery," I replied.

I felt the sun's warmth tickle my cheeks. My face was unhidden by the strands of unkempt hair that had sheltered my being. I had hidden behind them for far too long. I felt confident and alive, like the emergence of a new day or a glorious resurrection of my old self.

"I no longer feel shame," I said.

"You were never meant to feel shame. The shame you felt was merely a mask for the sadness that had overtaken your life," revealed Norman.

"So then, the feeling of shame was planted there by the world's monsters?"

"Yes, they convinced you that what you *had* or *had not* done was the reason for their inflicted scars. But truthfully, the fault was never yours. You were always a forest. They just made you doubt yourself with their malice, fear, and trauma" explained Norman.

I smiled and began to cry softly. In the comfort of my tears, I took rest, laying upon the ground. Emotions swirled within my very being, like a hurricane emerging from a stalled heart. I had believed their lies. I had blamed myself. But now I knew the abundant truth. I held no blame for the actions of the evil. I deserved no shame for the deeds of the wicked. There was only one truth I now held.

They were to blame.

I sat with this truth for a moment. It consoled me and I felt a sense of freedom.

"I wish to go back to my forest. Back to my comfort and self," I finally said.

"You will have to face those who have broken you," reminded Norman.

I smiled.

"Good. I have no fear. I will strike them down from their self-proclaimed thrones and burn them where they fall."

"Very well. Then you must travel back the way you came. You must relive your scars. And then you must face the monsters that wait for you. A warning though. Like with all newfound strengths, your courage may dim slightly as you take this journey."

"Will you accompany me?" I asked.

"I cannot be your strength," said Norman.

"Why not?"

"Because you already possess all the strength you need."

I looked at Norman sadly. I did not require them to be my strength. I simply longed for them to be my companion. Norman must have been able to read me clearer than I had thought was possible.

"Fine," said Norman. "I will go with you. *Not* as your strength. But as a friend and a reminder."

"A reminder of what?"

"That you were a forest."

I smiled and once again stood tall, immediately marching back into the forest that I had just traveled. Proudly. This was not merely a journey back to where I was. No, this was a battle cry that took me to a future that I deserved. And as Norman bounced about, at my side, I knew that I was destined for peace. I was destined for resolve. Even if that meant spilling the blood of those who had hurt me.

I marched on.

~ Chapter Eleven: Back the Way We Came ~

The day pressed hard against my aging steps. As if it were trying to push me backward, to a place where I could only live my life being mildly content, but not actually satisfied. Norman helped pull me forward by singing melodies and cheering me on. Norman may not have been my strength, but they were a small portion of what kept it alive. The strange little creature was simply that cool sip of water that I needed to keep going.

I felt like a giant, trouncing across the forest as if the trees were miles beneath me. I could feel my feet almost connect to the soil, allowing it to fuel my driving force. Unstoppable, with forward momentum, and not wavered by any natural discourse.

I was a giant.

I was a forest.

As I found myself being drawn deeper into the forest. I came across a familiar creature. A creature with two faces. A creature that I would quite like at my side while facing down those who had lived to harm me.

"Oh, look who it is again," remarked Face 1, sad as ever.

"Is it the confused girl?!" yelled Face 2, angry as ever.

"I am no longer confused," I announced rather proudly.

"And I must declare that I want to invite you both to accompany myself, and Norman, on my return journey."

"Why would you want two sad sods, such as us, to go with you?" asked Face 1.

"She is clearly *still* incredibly confused," remarked Face 2.

"Because, only through all kinds of grief, sad and angry, can we find ourselves in the presence of peace. You are both a necessary, albeit rather annoying, part of my process."

"Annoying you say?!" yelled Face 2.

"She's not wrong," said Face 1.

"She rarely is," Norman chimed in.

"Who's Norman?!" yelled Face 2.

   The trepidation-filled duo then chatted amongst themselves for several minutes. Routinely they both popped their heads up and looked over in my direction, which was somewhat odd since Face 2 did not possess eyes of any form. After a long while, Face 1 cleared their throat to speak.

"We will gladly join you on your journey," said Face 1.

They announced it within the slightest glimmer of happiness. Just a slice of the unfamiliar for this melancholy pair. Perhaps even within grief, hope can be found.

"I wouldn't say that we were *gladly going*," scoffed Face 2.

Through the forest, we marched. A flourishing army, building force and confidence like a growing storm. Far more aware of our own strengths than we all were prior. We were the weapons of nature that would reclaim back our lives. And just like a storm, we would strike without regret.

As we journeyed towards the fields of gray, we eventually entered the range of white trees. Their beauty lit our way, whispering to me of power and resolve. My fists clenched and my pace quickened as we approached the tree line, destined to come face to face with the monsters of my past. The monsters that had drug me here against my will and retired my youth to that of a jaded memory.

I could feel my fear trying to creep back up on me. Like an insect trying to burrow itself deep in my thoughts. I tried to shake off this feeling. I tried to hold onto my newfound courage. But with every step I took, I felt increasingly anxious about facing this evil.

Before I crossed the thin line of trees, into the fields, and back to the dead forest of my youth, I decided that I needed one more companion on this journey. For even in the darkest of times, one should never be wary of a kindhearted joke.

I slowly entered the hollow tree where I had first met Bee. There, unmoved, like a painting stuck in time, was Bee.

"Hello, Bee," I said.

Bee slowly turned towards me. There was a look of recollection in their open eyes. An almost glimmer of surprise and happiness radiated from their being.

"You look as if you have carved out a small bit of bliss from a frightening world."

"I have," I said with a smirk across my face. "And I owe *much* of it to you. For you were my first step on this journey."

"Knock, knock," said Bee.

"Who's there?" I replied.

"Tank,"

"Tank who?"

Bee rose from their chair and calmly, albeit slowly, made their way over to me.

"You are most welcome my friend," Bee said.

I chuckled slightly and gave this strange creature a gentle hug.

"You would like me to follow you into the depths of your past. That is why you have visited me, correct?" Bee asked.

"That is correct," I replied.

"It would be an honor," said Bee.

And so, through the gray fields, we traveled. A party of strangers and friends, all of whom had influenced my absolute potential. To be alive when others said I should not be. To be at peace when others said I should find no solace. A misfit army that roamed these lands, ready for anything, but not sure what to expect.

As we got closer to the forest of my youth, we began to fill a freezing fog creeping in all around us. It left us chilled to our traveling bones, and oh so tired. I could feel the three, just beyond the tree line, waiting for us. They sounded hungry as the air was filled with the growls and screeching of famished evil. Every step we took brought us closer and closer to destiny. Face to face with my damaged past and hopeful future. There are no words to describe the fear that one feels when ordained with the occasion to face those whom have left scars draped across your being and body. Such a chance is a very unwelcome rarity. But one that I did not plan on squandering.

Once we had made our way past the tree line, we found ourselves in a familiar clearing. I remembered meeting the three here before. When I was lost and searching for *any* type of reprieve. I remembered how they had mocked me. I remembered how they had hurt me. Damaged and tortured. My anger grew. I was ready to face them. But where were they? My patience had worn thin as I struggled to live within waiting. Now must be the time to fight their venom with that of my own. Frustrated, I looked about, behind every tree branch, beneath every stone.

"Where are they?" I yelled in a panicked tone.

My heart raced. If I could *not* face these monsters, then how could I ever move on? How could I embrace my new future if I did not kill the past? I paused for a moment. Perhaps this was a good thing. Maybe facing the past was unneeded. In the back of my mind, I was somehow relieved to not come face to face with… and there they were. As if beckoned by a thought. Face to face with the disjointed evil that had left so many scars strung across my body. Face to face with the Wolf.

~ Chapter Twelve: The Wolf ~

"I see you!" screamed the Wolf.

Their eyes were opened, deformed but soul-piercing, invading my *very* being. They caused my heart to race and contort like the nightmarish acrobatics of an apocalypse. Born of fire and death, surrounded by the sharpened teeth of a true apex predator. Gone was that feeling of being a giant. And just as I had felt when I was drug into this inverted realm, I once again felt weak and small. I fell to the ground and clutched my eyes shut. Sobbing and praying that this monster would leave me alone.

"Look at me," hissed the Wolf while approaching my tear-soaked face.

Blinded by the salt that clung to my cold cheeks I dared not reply. I would *not* look. I would spend all of eternity buried beneath my own emotions, only breathing when deemed absolutely necessary.

"I said… look at me!" repeated the Wolf.

"No," I whispered.

But then I felt a warm grip upon my hand. I had almost forgotten that my journey had been accompanied by my various strengths. Norman placed their reach within that of my own. I slowly opened my eyes to look upon the curious creature who had spent their night singing to me so that I could rest and then be reborn. Behind their kind face, I could just barely make out the shadow of the Wolf, hovering in place, waiting for me to surrender myself. But I maintained eye contact with Norman and clasped onto them the best I could. They helped me to my feet, escorted with kindness and a gentle breath.

"You were a forest," whispered Norman.

I clung to these whispered words and eventually found the strength to stand tall once more. My eyes still remained closed, but I breathed deep, clenched my fists, and let this embracing power from deep within devour the evil that had been planted within me by the Wolf and their brethren.

"They are rather terrifying," remarked Face 1.

"I've seen worse!" argued Face 2.

"Seen worse!?" screamed the Wolf. "I am all the evil that the world has *ever* known! You are all just swine!"

The two faces of lament just stood there speechless for a moment or two.

"Oh yes, we've definitely seen worse," remarked Face 2 with a little chuckle.

"You dare to mock me?!" snarled the Wolf.

"Yes…I think we dare," replied Face 1.

I smiled for a moment as my eyes wandered up to try and find the face of the Wolf. I could feel the fearful nature of my being begin to drift aside. If the two faces of lament could bravely mock this monster, then so could I.

"You're pathetic," I whispered.

"What was that?" asked the Wolf.

"I said…"

I stood tall and marched right up to the face of fear itself, just a breath away. And before the Wolf could say a word, I screamed.

"…You're pathetic!"

The Wolf jumped back from me and stumbled over their own cloak, spiraling to the ground in an almost comical display.

"See, told you we'd seen worse," laughed Face 2.

Bee slowly walked over to me and looked down at the laughable, pitiful monster that had been draped upon the forest floor. Just as I had been upon when I first arrived.

"Do you want to hear a riddle?" Bee asked the Wolf.

"No!" screamed the Wolf while trying to pull themselves up off the ground.

"Okay," started Bee. "I am the beginning of everything, the end of time and space, the beginning of every end, and the end of every place. What am I?"

Before the Wolf could reply, I dug down deep into my soul and summoned all the strength I had in me.

"Death," I whispered.

My arms unexpectedly transformed into two giant tree branches, hulking and sharp. I immediately stabbed the Wolf. A branch in each side of their chest. I was a forest, and these were my weapons. I was resolved to destroy what had left these pointless scars scattered upon my body and mind. The Wolf screamed and began wilting away to ash. Their shadows, now merely embers in the wind, their evil, washed away by the breeze. I was left in the presence of nothing but a painful memory of my attacker. They no longer had control of me. I fell to the ground and began to sob. Norman came to my side and comforted me so that I could gain back my composure.

"The answer wasn't death," Bee finally said after a few moments.

"What?" I asked while wiping my tears.

"The answer to the riddle. It wasn't death. It was the letter E," said Bee innocently.

I chuckled a little bit and rose once more to my feet.

"She was trying to be dramatic!" yelled Face 2.

I found though that my celebration was short-lived as I quickly realized that I had only struck down one of the three. I heard laughing in the distance of these dying woods. It was cynical and sharp. It was malice and apathetic. I knew that laugh.

"Where are you?!" I screamed.

The Ravenous then emerged from out of nowhere, appearing from nothing and finding themselves right in front of me. They did not seem to wear fear after seeing what I had just done to the Wolf.

"Why are you laughing?! I've slain your friend!"

"I have no friends!" screamed the Ravenous.

I peered around looking for the third, the Withered. The one that had helped me but had not asked for forgiveness. I planned to show no mercy to any of these three.

"Where is the other one?!" I asked.

"The Withered? They retired themselves to the great beyond out of shame and guilt. Like the coward that they were!"

"And after seeing both of your friends vanish to nothing, are you not afraid?!" I screamed.

I wanted this monster to feel fear. The way I had felt fear. The way *so* many before me had felt fear. There were no condolences that could *ever* be offered for what they had done to me.

"As I've already said, I have no friends!" the Ravenous screamed.

I could taste their ending upon my lips.

"Very well. Then no one will mourn you!" I replied.

I lunged at the monster with my bare hands and began to tear away at their shadowed self. Piece by piece ripping them apart. They screamed in pain while also laughing at the same time until their screams and laughing eventually disappeared to nothing but a memory. They were gone, and I was left with nothing but my own thoughts.

~ Chapter Thirteen: The Truth ~

I had vanquished my foes and demons, leaving myself embraced by the silence of the surrounding forest. I inhaled the cool air, taking it deep into my eager lungs. I waited for my mind and heart to fill with the overwhelming impression of happiness. I waited in silence for an assumption that did not come. Mysteriously, I found that I *still* felt somewhat weighed down by my own sadness. I *still* felt shame for something that should require no such dishonor. I had found my morality hidden with laughter, lament, and compassion. And with them at my side, I had struck the final, and fatal, blow to these monsters. The leavers of scars. The echoes left behind by the Wolf and the Ravenous as they fell from this realm to the next, still screamed at me from deep within my thoughts. Was it wrong to feel joy, knowing that they would never find peace? Should I feel shame? Should I feel…

"You must stop!" yelled Norman.

"What must I stop?" I replied.

"You should not feel *any* shame for the monsters which you have vanquished or what they did to you. They were predators from then, until now, until the end. Do not doubt that you were surely not their only victim. Leaving those types of scars across a soul such as yourself takes much practice."

How had Norman peered deep into the shadows of my mind and found out what was parading throughout my scattered thoughts? How was it that they knew *exactly* what I was thinking before having thought it?

"Knock, knock," whispered Bee.

This seemed an odd time for a joke.

"Who's there?" I whispered back.

"You," Bee replied.

And then, before I could reply, they all disappeared into nothing, vanishing into a breath. Norman, Bee, Face 1, and Face 2. Gone like the stars in a morning's light. They had left me all alone. Alone with my thoughts. Alone with my truths. But what were they? Strangely, I still felt their unwavering presence. I could still feel the warm touch of Norman. I could hear the awful jokes of Bee. I could quietly observe the hither and thither of bickering between the faces of lament. Although they had vanished, it was like they were still here, surrounding my frail being. And then I felt a thought form. A simple thought. One which I should have been painfully aware of throughout my most impractical journey.

"It's me. This… is *all* me," I whispered.

The ground unexpectedly began to tremble violently as cracks erupted from the soil below my tired feet. A void opened up from the middle of this deceased forest, and from deep within the ground arose a giant structure.

Slowly it climbed up to the sky, just outside of my immediate gaze. It was taller than any tree, and at its top sat an orb. Illuminating the forest and blinding my limited contemplation. I found it impossible to illustrate its appearance, for just like an unspoken truth, it is rather impossible to describe. The trees that surrounded it began to rise and wake. Their limbs outstretched as if this orb was offering them rebirth and new life. The trees were desperate for this resurrection, but the orb did not acknowledge them. It hummed and buzzed, shaking the ground. It was almost the reverberation one might feel and hear after striking a massive bell with a giant mallet. But what was I perceiving? Was all of this actually my creation? Were the ones that I had met on my journey merely the limbs of a lost forest?

I cautiously approached this tower that was reaching for the heavens. Unsure of what to do or say. But part of me, buried deep below my fading breath, felt that I should speak to this tower as if it were simply alive. I perceived no ears from its side, but I knew it would hear my timid voice.

"Hello!" I yelled as loud as I could.

"Hello," the tower replied.

What was this voice? It sounded so *very* familiar. So *very* kind. So *very*…me. It was my own voice replying. An echo that perplexed and confused me.

"Who are you?" I asked.

"I am you. From your past and future, but never from your present. I am your aspirations and needed fears. A mind's eye of what you long to be."

"And what is it that I long to be?"

"You long to be seen. You long to be heard. You long to survive, turn back the hands of time, and find a home where you can bury your roots deep in the soil."

"Is that not the wish of everyone and everything?" I asked.

"Perhaps, but accomplishing such things is easier for others. For they may not have the same demons to battle as yourself."

"I vanquished my demons!" I yelled.

"Yes, all of those evils. Except for the last one."

  My heart dropped. Last one? What was I referring to? I had destroyed the Wolf and the Ravenous. And the Withered had destroyed themselves because their guilt was far too much to handle. So, what was this last evil?

"Your own shame!" the tower screamed.

"My own shame?"

"Yes! You *still* feel guilt and shame. As if you should be trapped by remorse for having found yourself here! You *still* believe that your choices are why you are here! You *still* believe that you should feel regrets for finding joy in the vanquishing of those monsters!"

"And should I not?! I pushed the button! I traveled the hall! I hid in the dying forest! I smiled at the monster's demise! My choices brought me here! My choices defined me!" I argued.

"But their choices are the only ones that matter when it comes to feelings of shame," said the tower.

"But I…" I had no words.

"Your shame needs to be exiled. You were the prey. You… *we*, are the victim."

I fell to the ground, speechless, as the tears filled my eyes, ready to dive from their mountain top and deep into the forest's floor. I could see the monsters of my past, painted beautifully, just beyond the horizon. And yet, still somehow mocking me from beyond their eternal and tormented destiny.

"You *must* destroy the part of yourself that wants to blame you!" screamed the tower before slowly and violently sinking back into the ground, their voice fading to nothing.

Once again, the tower was covered by this familiar dead soil, leaving me to my own resolve. My thoughts spun around as the sun began to set. The perspective vanished, taking the monsters of my past with it, and I was left in pure darkness, alone and bewildered. What was the next step to take? What was the revelation to adorn? And how could I rid myself of the shame that still found itself buried deep within my hollow coil?

The forest was silent and cold. Dead and alone. I had vanquished all, I had met many strange and curious creatures along the way. But now, abandoned, I was left unmoved and frightened. My eyes were closed tight as I drifted into a form of eternal sleep. I was there for what felt like a lifetime but was most likely simply a moment or two. I was there until something peculiar happened. An instant. A split second. A solitary star that appeared from the heavens, warming my shadowed face. I tilted my head towards where I thought it might be, brushed my weathered hair to the side, and after a long moment, I opened my eyes.

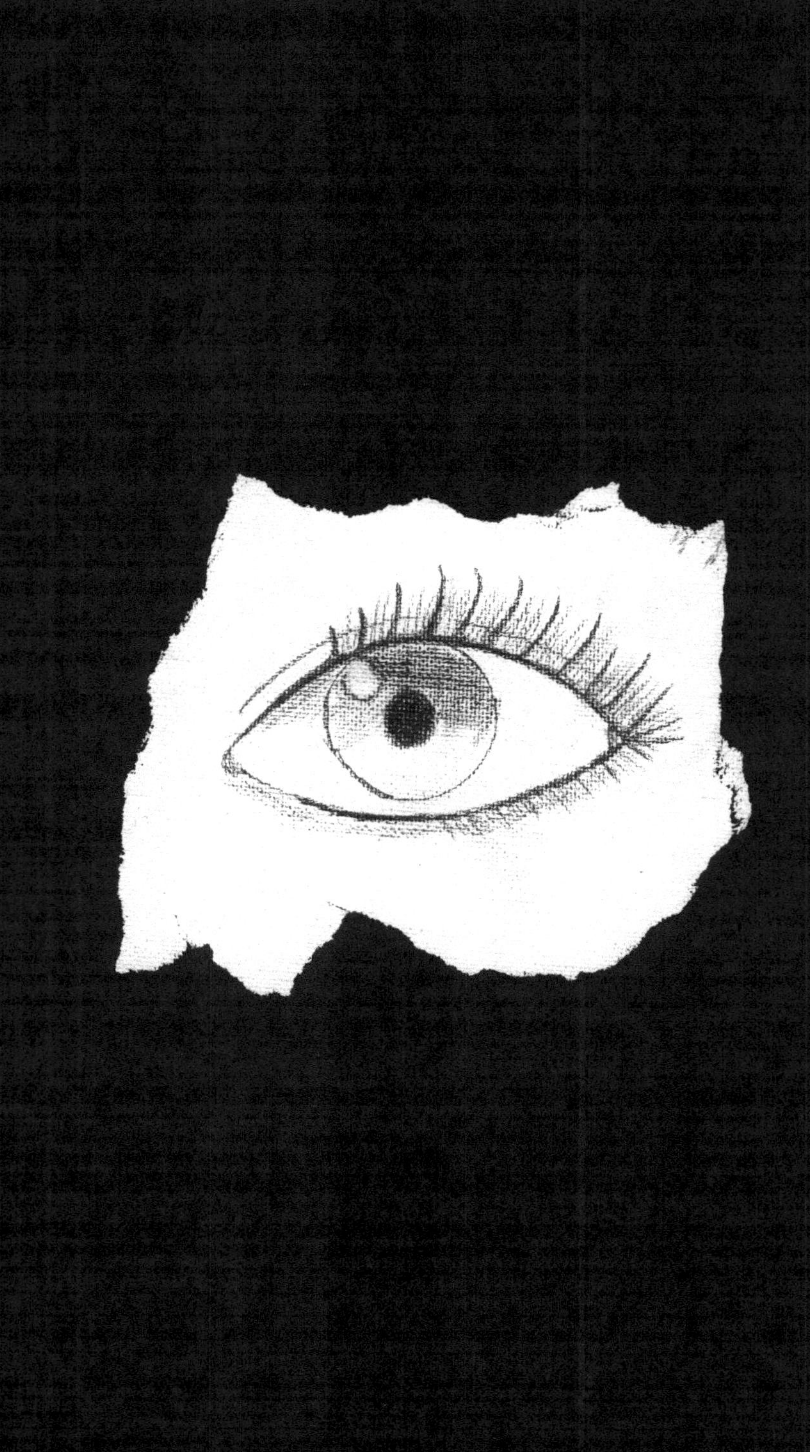

~ Chapter Fourteen: I... ~

Once upon a time, I *was* a forest.

I was born, innocent and frail, a gift to this world. An empty book with many chapters to be written. When I was young, I was told that I could be anything I wanted to be when I was grown. Those older than me had promised such things. For example, they promised that I could cross oceans and see the world. I was told that I could be anybody or do anything that my heart so desired. But, as with what happens with most of us when we grow older, reality rears its ugly head and reminds us of the heartless nature of this cruel world. This truth brought me sadness, and I ran away from those who had raised me. I tried to find a life that could bring me some kind of happiness.

I wandered this realm in search of freedom and love. In search of an unknown dream. Eventually, I found myself tired and distraught, worn down to the point of solitude. Then I had a revelation. Perhaps being content and restful was worth more than chasing the dreams of my youth. Perhaps the sadness that was ripped from an unfinished journey was not worth the steps taken. So, I found a place to rest. A safe place. And there, alone, in that place of rest and safety, I was attacked by three evils. Their intentions and actions were unspeakable and disgusting. Despicable creatures who chose to carry out appalling acts. But as I was left there, broken, and covered with scars both physically and mentally, I was made to feel shame. Why would I feel shame? I was left damaged and destroyed. A victim of trauma whose attackers faded into obscurity. I could still see the three. I could feel the one that laughed at my pain. I could see the one with those piercing and evil eyes. And I could hear the one that opted to question their unspeakable acts.

I hated them. I hated them all. I hated them for what they did to me.

So, drowning in unwarranted shame, and buried in anger, I retreated into the shadows. I was constantly haunted by the faces of those who had wronged me. I shut down. I forgot how to laugh, how to grieve, and how to trust. Time seemed to stand still.

A journey had to be taken.

I needed to remember the importance of a smile. I had to tell myself that no matter the anguish, I had to push myself to discover moments of happiness. It felt strange to find a chuckle every now and then after having endured so *very* much. But there was no reason to feel guilt when finding moments of joy.

A journey had to be taken.

I needed to grieve. I needed to be okay with being unhappy at one moment, and angry within the next. I needed to grasp the notion that there is no right or wrong way to grieve. To work through the pains of the past is not an ending process. It takes time. I would always find myself overtaken by those moments of sadness and anger. But I would try to accept those moments for what they were, part of the process.

A journey had to be taken.

I needed to trust again. Every shadow scared me. Every stilted breath felt dangerous. But I would learn to trust, and love, and care. I would learn to open myself up to strangers and trust the world when trust was earned.

A journey had to be taken.

I needed to kill the past. And when those monsters were finally found, two were condemned and made absent. My hatred was okay to have. My anger was okay to bare. The third of the three could not live with what had been done and had chosen to retire their own existence. I could never forgive. But I could grieve for the lives that could have once been. Defined by the aged realities and not by the child's eyes.

A journey had to be taken.

I needed to feel better, but I still felt shame. Why did the words and actions of this world make me feel as though I should carry this shame throughout my life? Why was it my burden? It should not be. But I felt embarrassed to talk about it. I felt as though the souls that I put trust in would look at me as broken. Who could ever love a soul so damaged?

I stood in darkness, aside from the one star that lit this shadowed forest. I was alone. Should not these traveled feet feel at peace after such a journey? Should not my heart be full of love and acceptance now that my demons had met their fate? It made no sense as to why I could not simply move on.

I wept.

Tears flowed from my eyes. Like a dam that was slowly breaking. I screamed at the heavens, questioning why. I screamed of hate and betrayal. I screamed of loss and innocence. And as these tears began to flow like a river and be drunk up by this lifeless forest floor, something amazing happened. The sky began to shimmer with stars, bright and warm, lighting up the limbs and soil that surrounded my figure.

Suddenly, the grounds erupted with soft grasses and the trees began to sprout leaves and flowers, as if they had drunk my tears and deserted their thirst, finding new life and rebirth. It happened so quickly that I found myself not able to breathe or fathom what I was observing. What was this? What was happening? And then, it became clearer than it had before. I lived in a past that longed for the future. These scars. These horrible scars. They were mine to carry. But nothing to ever be ashamed of. Nothing anyone should be ashamed of.

I smiled. I felt joy. It had snuck in between my grieving moments and made a home for itself deep within my soul. I slept. I rested. I woke. I lived. And then I did it again, and again. I wore my scars, and I faced them with courage. For I had assembled the greatest truth that I could have ever fathomed.

I remembered back to when I was young. An unwritten book. And as I continued to live, I repeated the following in my head again and again.

I AM strong.

I AM beautiful.

I AM life.

I AM love.

I AM a survivor.

I *was* a forest…

NO.

I AM A FOREST.

The End

Thank you for reading and coming along on this journey!

If you enjoyed this story, please check out these other works by Nathan Harms.

Until next time, dear reader.

Interra

Paperback:979-8-7216-7342-9
Hardcover:979-8-5040-4812-3

I Was a Forest

Paperback:979-8-4259-5967-6
Hardcover:979-8-4259-6474-8

Good Bird

Paperback:979-8-8315-9860-5
Hardcover:979-8-8315-9922-0

The Theory of Thought

Paperback:979-8-8488-7328-3
Hardcover:979-8-8488-7353-5